All-Star Players™

# MEET LADAINIAN TOMLINSON

## Football's Fastest Running Back

Ethan Edwards



PowerKiDS press™
New York

Published in 2009 by The Rosen Publishing Group, Inc.
29 East 21st Street, New York, NY 10010



First Edition

Editor: Amelie von Zumbusch
Book Design: Greg Tucker
Photo Researcher: Jessica Gerweck

Photo Credits: Cover, pp. 4, 7, 9, 10, 14, 15, 17, 18, 19, 20, 22, 23, 25, 26, 27, 29, 30 © Getty Images; p. 11 © AFP/Getty Images; p. 12 © TSN/Icon SMI.

Library of Congress Cataloging-in-Publication Data

Edwards, Ethan.
Meet LaDainian Tomlinson : football's fastest running back / Ethan Edwards. — 1st ed.
p. cm. — (All-star players)
Includes index.
ISBN 978-1-4042-4491-7 (library binding)
1. Tomlinson, LaDainian—Juvenile literature. 2. Football players—United States—Biography—Juvenile literature. I. Title.
GV939.T65E39 2009
796.332092—dc22
[B]

2008007564

Manufactured in the United States of America

# Contents

LaDainian Tomlinson wears a dark visor that keeps the sunlight out of his eyes while he is playing football.

# Meet LaDainian Tomlinson

LaDainian Tomlinson is one of the most humble players in the NFL, or National Football League. Some famous **athletes** are known for having big mouths, but Tomlinson is not one of them. Tomlinson is a running back for the San Diego Chargers. A running back's job is to run with the football toward the other team's end zone. This is called rushing.

Tomlinson does not need to talk about himself. He is one of the best rushers in the history of the NFL. His playing speaks for itself. Tomlinson is one of the best running backs ever to step onto a football field!

## All-Star Facts

**Tomlinson is often known by his nickname, L. T.**

Tomlinson was born in Rosebud, Texas, on June 23, 1979. His father, Oliver, loved football. Some of Tomlinson's earliest memories are of watching and playing football with his father. When he was seven years old, LaDainian's parents divorced. After that, LaDainian did not see his father very often. LaDainian's mother, Loreane, raised the family by herself. However, football was still important to LaDainian. It reminded him of his father.

LaDainian Tomlinson was such a good athlete that he played several positions on his high-school football team. He often played against a young **quarterback** named Drew Brees. The two young players soon became good friends.

## All-Star Facts

**LaDainian has a sister, Londria, and a brother, LaVar.**

Tomlinson (right) and Brees (left) remained good friends and continued to play football together in the years after they finished high school.

# The Horned Frogs

Tomlinson knew he was good enough to play football for a major college. Unfortunately, the big college **scouts** did not believe he had enough experience playing running back. This meant that the big colleges were not interested in him. Several smaller schools were interested in him, though. Tomlinson picked Texas Christian University because his mother lived nearby.

Texas Christian's football team is called the Horned Frogs. They were terrible! However, it did not take Tomlinson long to help turn the team around. In Tomlinson's sophomore, or second, year, the Horned Frogs reached the Sun Bowl. This is an important college football game that happens every year in El Paso, Texas.

*Tomlinson (center) broke Texas Christian University's records for both scoring and rushing in his time there.*

WAC
TCU

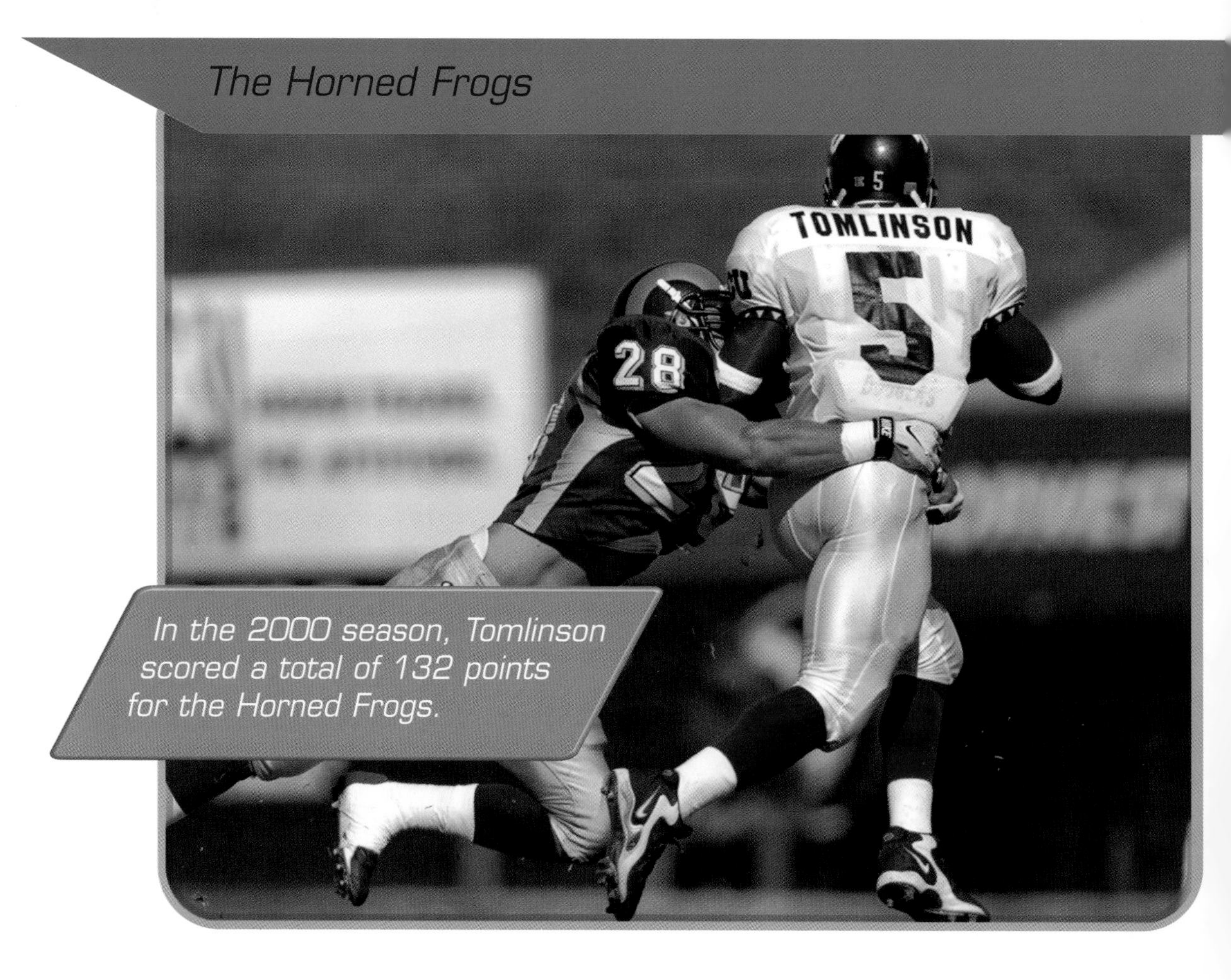


In the 2000 season, Tomlinson scored a total of 132 points for the Horned Frogs.

Tomlinson was the nation's leading college rusher in his last two years. He came in fourth in the voting for the Heisman Trophy, a prize awarded each year to the best **offensive** college player. Tomlinson had become one of the best young running backs in the nation, and football **experts** were finally paying attention.

Tomlinson worked so hard at improving his football skills that he was not able to complete his college **degree**. This bothered him because he values education. Although he decided to try out for the NFL without finishing college, Tomlinson promised his mother that he would someday earn a college degree.

*Tomlinson (second from left) and his fellow Heisman Trophy finalists laughed together at this December 2000 party.*

iXCEL
WAC

# The 2001 NFL Draft

The NFL draft happens every year. The draft is a system that NFL teams use to select new, young players. There are 32 teams in the NFL. All 32 teams take turns choosing one player in each round of the draft. The best players are generally selected during the first round. First-round players get lots of money. They are expected to become **starters** for their new teams. Teams that finished the season with bad records get to choose before teams that finished with good records. This means that bad teams have better chances to pick the best players. The NFL draft is a system that allows teams to improve.

*Tomlinson's great record with Texas Christian University meant that Tomlinson was likely to be one of the early first-round picks in the 2001 NFL Draft.*

LaDainian Tomlinson happily showed off a Chargers uniform when he appeared with NFL commissioner, or head, Paul Tagliabue at the 2001 NFL Draft.

The San Diego Chargers finished the 2000 season with a terrible record. They needed a good young player who could make the team better. The Chargers had watched Tomlinson's college career very closely. They thought he could help their team.

The Chargers had the fifth pick in the first round of the draft. They hoped that none of the first four teams would choose Tomlinson. The Chargers were in luck and drafted Tomlinson in the first round of the 2001 NFL Draft. In the second round, they drafted Tomlinson's friend Drew Brees. The good friends were now on the same team!

*The Chargers were delighted to have Tomlinson join them. The team needed a good running back very badly.*

# On the Rise

Most NFL players do not become starters early in their first season. Even college stars need time to learn how to play in the more **competitive** NFL. However, Tomlinson did not get much time. The Chargers needed him badly, so he became the starting running back in his first season.

In his very first game, Tomlinson surprised his team and the football world by rushing for 113 yards! A game with 100 or more rushing yards is a good game for a running back. As it turned out, Tomlinson's 113 yards was just the start of a wonderful **rookie** season.

*After joining the Chargers, Tomlinson chose to wear the number 21. He picked it because it comes between 20 and 22, the numbers worn by the great running backs Barry Sanders and Emmitt Smith.*

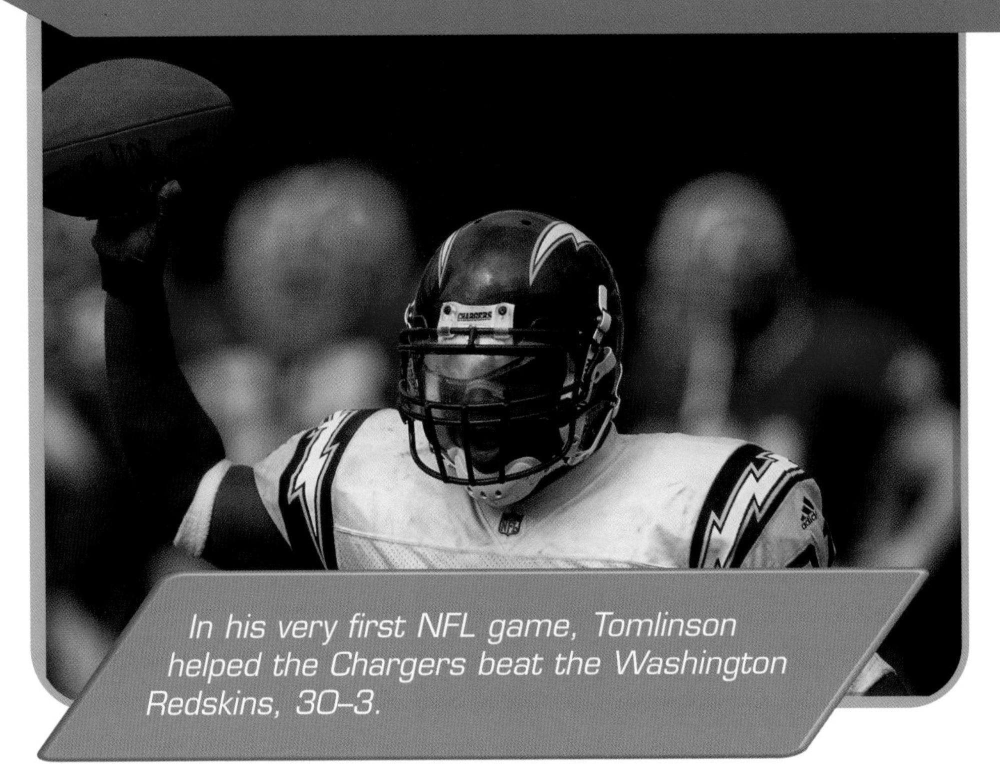

In his very first NFL game, Tomlinson helped the Chargers beat the Washington Redskins, 30–3.

Running backs usually try to reach a total of 1,000 yards in a season. Tomlinson **eclipsed** this goal in his rookie season with a total of 1,236 yards! He even got to play against his childhood **idol** Emmitt Smith in a game against the Dallas Cowboys. The San Diego Chargers finished the season with a losing record, but the fans were excited. They knew that Tomlinson could lead their team to greatness!

Tomlinson played even harder in his second season. He set a Chargers record by running for a total of 1,683 yards. No other player in team history had ever run that far in one season.

*In 2002, Tomlinson's hard work and will to win convinced his fellow Chargers to name Tomlinson the team's Offensive Player of the Year.*

# L. T. Is MVP

Tomlinson quickly became known as one of the best running backs in the NFL. In 2003, he scored nearly half of the Chargers' total points by himself! In 2004, the rest of the Chargers began to play well, too. They had their first winning season in nine years, and Tomlinson and Brees led the team into the **play-offs**.

Tomlinson made NFL history in 2005. He set a new NFL record by running for at least one touchdown in 14 games in a row. However, he was just warming up for the next season.

In 2006, Tomlinson broke 13 NFL records and 6 Chargers records. He was also the NFL's leading rusher. This means that no other running back in

*In the 2005 season, Tomlinson scored 20 touchdowns. That was the most touchdowns that any member of the Chargers had ever made in a single season.*

After Tomlinson broke an NFL record by scoring 29 touchdowns during the 2006 season, his teammates lifted him up into the air to celebrate.

the entire NFL ran for more yards than Tomlinson did that year. Tomlinson also set an NFL record that year by becoming the first player to score 186 points in a single season.

America's football **journalists** elected the record-setting Tomlinson the regular season's Most Valuable Player, or MVP. He received many more votes than any other player did. That same season, Tomlinson also went to his fifth Pro Bowl, a special game in which only the best players in the NFL can play. The magazine *Sports Illustrated* named Tomlinson "the greatest player in the NFL."

*In 2005, Tomlinson's touchdown helped the AFC, or American Football Conference, beat the NFC, or National Football Conference, in the Pro Bowl.*

# Off the Football Field

Family life is important to Tomlinson. He met his wife, LaTorsha, while they were in college. The Tomlinsons go out on a date at least once a week. They live in San Diego, California, with three dogs, named Coco, Fendi, and Sweetness. Coco is a teacup poodle, and Fendi is a terrier. Sweetness, a pit bull, was named after Walter Payton, one of Tomlinson's heroes. Payton was one of the best running backs in NFL history, and Sweetness was his nickname.

In his free time, Tomlinson likes watching basketball. He is a fan of the Los Angeles Lakers. Tomlinson also loves old cars. He owns a bright red 1964 Chevrolet Impala.

## All-Star Facts

**LaDainian Tomlinson's favorite movie is the football film *Remember the Titans*.**

LaDainian and LaTorsha Tomlinson were married in 2003. LaDainian is generally quiet, but LaTorsha is talkative and outgoing.

Many sports stars are **criticized** for being spoiled and making too much money. Tomlinson knows that it is important to use his money to give back to the community. He and his wife created an organization, called Tomlinson's Touching Lives Foundation. The foundation is a **charity** that raises

*LaDainian Tomlinson enjoys other sports besides football. He particularly likes basketball. In 2007, he even took part in the McDonald's NBA All-Star Celebrity Game.*

money to help young people in San Diego and Texas. It provides more than 1,500 Christmas gifts to sick children in San Diego hospitals.

The foundation also awards 30 **scholarships** every year with the L. T. School Is Cool Scholarship Fund. It chooses 15 students from San Diego and 15 students from Tomlinson's old high school in Texas.

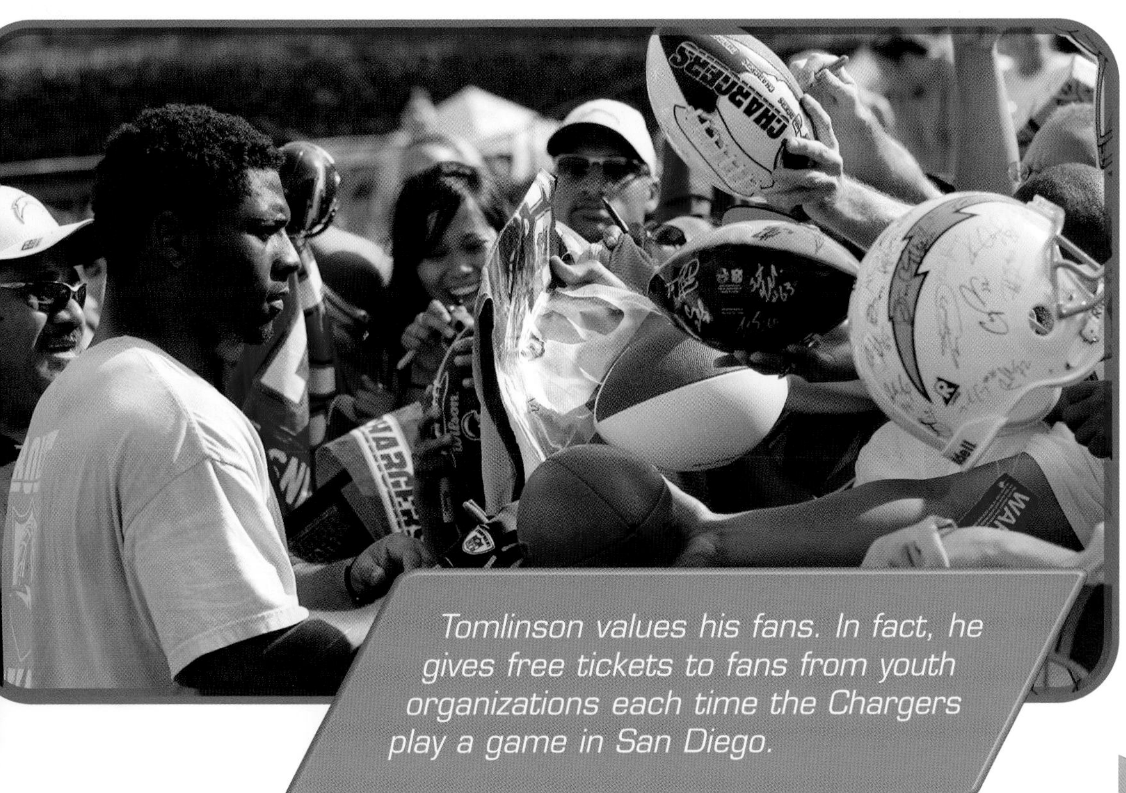

*Tomlinson values his fans. In fact, he gives free tickets to fans from youth organizations each time the Chargers play a game in San Diego.*

# L. T. Keeps Promises

In 2005, Tomlinson kept the promise he had made to his mother and received his degree from Texas Christian University. The life of an NFL star is busy, but Tomlinson worked hard to make time to complete his studies. Tomlinson knows that football is not the only important thing in life. He values education, hard work, and helping others.

Tomlinson helped the San Diego Chargers become one of the NFL's best teams. He hopes that someday he will help them win the Super Bowl. Unlike many athletes who always talk about themselves, Tomlinson shows off only on the field.

*Many sports experts agree that Tomlinson is the best running back playing today. Some even say he is one of the best running backs of all time.*

CHARGERS
21

# Stat Sheet

Height: 5' 10" (1.8 m)
Weight: 221 pounds (100 kg)
Team: San Diego Chargers
Position: Running back
Uniform Number: 21
Date of Birth: June 23, 1979

## 2007 Season Stats

| Yards | Rushing Touchdowns | Fumbles |
|---|---|---|
| 1,474 | 15 | 0 |

## Career Stats as of the 2007 Season

| Yards | Rushing Touchdowns | Fumbles |
|---|---|---|
| 10,650 | 115 | 24 |